THE
TURMERIC
COOKBOOK

A COLLECTION OF THE MOST
UNIQUE TURMERIC RECIPES

By
Umm Maryam
Copyright © 2015 by Saxonberg
Associates

Published by
BookSumo, a division of Saxonberg
Associates
http://www.booksumo.com/

A GIFT FROM ME TO YOU...

Send the Book!

Hey thanks for purchasing my cookbook. If you join my private reader's club you will get one of my favorite books: *A Kitchen in Morocco: Classical Moroccan Recipes.*

This cookbook has over 35 amazing Moroccan and West African recipes that you will absolutely LOVE! It is not available to anyone else, except private readers.

You'll learn how to make classical Moroccan Cous Cous, Peanut Stews, Tagine, Cous Cous Kebabs and a lot more. So join my club!

You will also receive updates about all my new books when they are free. So please show your support.

Also don't forget to like and subscribe on the social networks. I love meeting my readers. Links to all my profiles are below so please click and connect :)

Facebook

Twitter

Google +

ABOUT THE AUTHOR.

Umm Maryam is a self-proclaimed lover of culture. She focuses her time on writing books about different countries in the Arab and Asian world.

For a complete listing of all my books please see my author page.

INTRODUCTION

Thank you for purchasing my *Secret Turmeric Cookbook: A Collection of the Most Unique Turmeric Recipes.*

So why turmeric you may be asking yourself?

The reason is the health benefits!

If you are not trying to use turmeric as much as possible in your cooking you are honestly missing out on some amazing health benefits that you may not know of.

The secret to turmeric is the natural nutrient called curcumin. This curcumin occurs in nature and it is what gives turmeric its beautiful yellow colour.

The natural nutrient is quite possibly the most powerful anti-inflammatory you can find.

This amazing spice will not only add a unique colour and taste to your foods any inflammation occurring in your body will immediately start to decrease when your digestive system begins to process the turmeric you ate.

Turmeric is one of the reasons spicy Indo-Asian cuisines are good for you.

Any problems you may face due to inflammation like certain forms of arthritis can possibly be lessened simply because of this spice.

Now I know this is a cookbook and not a diet book.

But it is important that you understand why I took the time to compile this cookbook and gather all the turmeric recipes I know of.

It is important for you to understand exactly how these turmeric recipes can help you and your family.

Now I'm not a doctor. I'm just a master-chef like you

;)

I just believe in natural medicine and that there is a cure for every ailment somewhere in nature, we just have to find it.

If you do not believe me and you want proof then look at the references section at the end of this cookbook where I have compiled some links for the skeptics.

In any case if you enjoyed, *The Secret Curry Cookbook* (check my author page), you absolutely will love *The Secret Turmeric Cookbook*.

This cookbook will teach you how to infuse this amazing spice into your cooking and into your life. To get some of the health benefits.

So I hope you are excited and motivated to try some new things! Now let's get started on this turmeric adventure!

--Umm Maryam

TABLE OF CONTENTS

ANY ISSUES? CONTACT ME

If you find that something important to you is missing from this book please contact me at umm@booksumo.com.

I will try my best to re-publish a revised copy taking your feedback into consideration and let you know when the book has been revised with you in mind.

:)

— Umm Maryam

NOTICE TO PRINT READERS:

Hey, because you purchased the print version of this book you are entitled to its original digital version for free by Amazon.

So when you have the time, please review your purchases, and download the Kindle version of this book.

You might enjoy consuming this book more in its original digital format.

;)

But, in any case, take care and enjoy reading in whatever format you choose!

LEGAL NOTES

COMMON ABBREVIATIONS

cup(s)	C.
tablespoon	tbsp
teaspoon	tsp
ounce	oz
pound	lb

*All units used are standard American measurements

CHAPTER 1: RECIPES FOR INFUSING TURMERIC INTO YOUR MEALS

RAISIN RICE

Ingredients

- 1 tbsp vegetable oil
- 1 1/2 C. basmati rice
- 1 (14 oz.) can coconut milk
- 1 1/4 (14 oz.) cans chicken stock
- 1/2 tsp ground cumin
- 1/2 tsp ground coriander
- 1 pinch mashed red pepper flakes
- 1 tsp salt
- 1/4 tsp ground turmeric
- 1 bay leaf
- 1/2 C. raisins
- 3/4 C. cashew halves

Directions

- Cook rice in hot oil for 2 minutes and add coconut milk, raisins, chicken stock, cumin, turmeric, coriander, red pepper flakes, salt, bay leaf and cashew halves before bringing all this to boil and cooking on low heat for 20 minutes.
- Serve.

Serving: 6

Timing Information:

Preparation	Cooking	Total Time
5 mins	22 mins	27 mins

Nutritional Information:

Calories	462 kcal
Carbohydrates	55.8 g
Cholesterol	2 mg
Fat	25.1 g
Fiber	2.2 g
Protein	8.4 g
Sodium	792 mg

* Percent Daily Values are based on a 2,000 calorie diet.

☐

Chicken Tikka Masala I

Ingredients

- 2 tbsps ghee (clarified butter)
- 1 onion, finely diced
- 4 cloves garlic, minced
- 1 tbsp ground cumin
- 1 tsp salt
- 1 tsp ground ginger
- 1 tsp cayenne pepper
- 1/2 tsp ground cinnamon
- 1/4 tsp ground turmeric
- 1 (14 oz.) can tomato sauce
- 1 C. heavy whipping cream
- 2 tsps paprika
- 1 tbsp white sugar
- 1 tbsp vegetable oil
- 4 skinless, boneless chicken breast halves, cut into bite-size pieces
- 1/2 tsp curry powder
- 1/2 tsp salt, or to taste(optional)
- 1 tsp white sugar, or to taste (optional)

Directions

- Cook onion in hot oil for 5 minutes and add garlic, and cook for another one minute before adding tsp salt, cinnamon, ginger, cayenne pepper and turmeric, and cooking everything for two minutes.
- Now stir in tomato sauce and bring everything to boil before cooking on low heat for ten minutes.
- Now add cream, paprika, and 1 tbsp sugar, and cook for another 15 minutes before cooking chicken and curry powder in hot oil for three minutes and transferring it into the sauce.
- Cook chicken in this sauce for 30 minutes.
- Serve.

Serving: 6

Timing Information:

Preparation	Cooking	Total Time
15 mins	1 hr 5 mins	1 hr 20 mins

Nutritional Information:

Calories	328 kcal
Carbohydrates	13.2 g
Cholesterol	106 mg
Fat	23.4 g
Fiber	2.3 g
Protein	17.9 g
Sodium	980 mg

* Percent Daily Values are based on a 2,000 calorie diet.

☐

OKRA

Ingredients

- 1 tbsp butter
- 3 onions, sliced
- 1 pound fresh okra, sliced in 1/8 inch pieces
- 1 1/2 tsps ground turmeric

Directions

- Cook onion in hot butter for a few minutes and then okra and turmeric before cooking it for 15 minutes or until you see that okra is tender.
- Serve.

Serving: 8

Timing Information:

Preparation	Cooking	Total Time
5 mins	15 mins	20 mins

Nutritional Information:

Calories	44 kcal
Carbohydrates	6.6 g
Cholesterol	4 mg
Fat	1.7 g
Fiber	2.3 g
Protein	1.7 g
Sodium	15 mg

* Percent Daily Values are based on a 2,000 calorie diet.

☐

EGGPLANT

Ingredients

- 1 eggplant
- 2 tbsps vegetable oil
- 1/2 tsp cumin seeds
- 1 medium onion, sliced
- 1 tsp diced fresh ginger
- 1 large tomato - peeled, seeded and diced
- 1 clove garlic, minced
- 1/2 tsp ground turmeric
- 1/2 tsp ground cumin
- 1/2 tsp ground coriander
- 1/4 tsp cayenne pepper
- 1/2 tsp salt, or to taste
- ground black pepper to taste
- 1/4 C. diced fresh cilantro

Directions

- Heat up your oven's broil.

- Broil egg planted coated with oil for 30 minutes and slice it into half before scrapping the flesh from its skin and slicing it into small pieces.
- Cook cumin seeds for a few seconds and add onion, garlic and ginger before cooking everything for a few more minutes.
- Cook for another few minutes after adding tomato, and season with turmeric, cayenne pepper, ground cumin, ground coriander, salt and black pepper.
- Stir in eggplant and cook for 15 minutes before garnishing it with fresh cilantro.
- Serve.

Serving: 4

Timing Information:

Preparation	Cooking	Total Time
15 mins	50 mins	1 hr 5 mins

Nutritional Information:

Calories	119 kcal
Carbohydrates	13.4 g
Cholesterol	0 mg
Fat	7.4 g
Fiber	6.1 g
Protein	2.4 g
Sodium	300 mg

* Percent Daily Values are based on a 2,000 calorie diet.

EASY DELICIOUS RICE

Ingredients

- 3 tbsps butter
- 1/2 onion, minced
- 2 cloves garlic, minced
- 2 C. chicken stock
- 1 C. brown rice
- 1 tsp curry powder
- 1/4 tsp ground turmeric
- 1/2 tsp dried thyme
- 1 bay leaf

Directions

- Cook onion and garlic in hot butter for 5 minutes before stirring in brown rice, thyme, curry powder, turmeric, bay leaf and boiling hot chicken stock.
- Turn down the heat to low and cook for 40 minutes.
- Serve.

Serving: 4

Timing Information:

Preparation	Cooking	Total Time
15 mins	40 mins	55 mins

Nutritional Information:

Calories	225 kcal
Carbohydrates	30.7 g
Cholesterol	23 mg
Fat	10.1 g
Fiber	2.7 g
Protein	3.5 g
Sodium	407 mg

* Percent Daily Values are based on a 2,000 calorie diet.

CURRY CAULIFLOWER

Ingredients

- 1 head cauliflower, cut into florets
- 2 tbsps vegetable oil
- 1 tsp salt
- 1 tbsp butter, cut into small pieces
- 1 large yellow onion, diced
- 1 tsp diced garlic
- 1 tsp curry powder
- 1 tsp cayenne pepper
- 1 tsp ground turmeric
- 1 quart chicken stock
- 1 C. heavy whipping cream
- salt and ground black pepper to taste
- 2 tbsps diced fresh parsley

Directions

- Set your oven at 450 degrees F before doing anything else.

- Bake cauliflower coated with vegetable oil and salt in the preheated oven for about 25 minutes.
- Cook onion in hot oil for 5 minutes and another 2 minutes after adding garlic.
- Now stir in curry powder, cayenne pepper and ground turmeric, and cooking everything for 5 more minutes before adding baked cauliflower and stock into the pan, and bringing everything to boil.
- Now cook on low heat for 10 minutes before blending everything in a food processor.
- Stir in some cream before serving in bowls.

Serving: 4

Timing Information:

Preparation	Cooking	Total Time
15 mins	50 mins	1 hr 5 mins

Nutritional Information:

Calories	359 kcal
Carbohydrates	15.1 g
Cholesterol	90 mg
Fat	32.7 g
Fiber	4.8 g
Protein	5.4 g
Sodium	1391 mg

* Percent Daily Values are based on a 2,000 calorie diet.

☐

GINGER CHILI CHICKEN

Ingredients

- 8 chicken thighs
- 4 tomatoes, quartered
- 8 cloves garlic, minced
- 4 tsps minced fresh ginger root
- 1 tsp chili powder
- 1 pinch ground turmeric
- 1 tsp salt
- 1/2 tsp coconut oil(optional)

Directions

- Cook mixture of chicken, chili powder, tomatoes, garlic, ginger, turmeric and salt over high heat until chicken turns brown and cook for another 45 minutes over low heat to get the chicken tendered.

Serving: 4

Timing Information:

Preparation	Cooking	Total Time
15 mins	50 mins	1 hr 5 mins

Nutritional Information:

Calories	326 kcal
Carbohydrates	5.4 g
Cholesterol	106 mg
Fat	19.8 g
Fiber	0.8 g
Protein	30.2 g
Sodium	770 mg

* Percent Daily Values are based on a 2,000 calorie diet.

CHICKEN CURRY I

Ingredients

- 2 pounds skinless, boneless chicken breast halves
- 2 tsps salt
- 1/2 C. cooking oil
- 1 1/2 C. diced onion
- 1 tbsp minced garlic
- 1 1/2 tsps minced fresh ginger root
- 1 tbsp curry powder
- 1 tsp ground cumin
- 1 tsp ground turmeric
- 1 tsp ground coriander
- 1 tsp cayenne pepper
- 1 tbsp water
- 1 (15 oz.) can mashed tomatoes
- 1 C. plain yogurt
- 1 tbsp diced fresh cilantro
- 1 tsp salt
- 1/2 C. water
- 1 tsp garam masala
- 1 tbsp diced fresh cilantro

- 1 tbsp fresh lemon juice

Directions

- Cook chicken breasts coated with salt in hot oil until brown and set it aside for later use.
- Cook onion, garlic and ginger in the same skillet for about 8 minutes and add curry powder, cayenne, cumin, turmeric, coriander and 1 tbsp of water before cooking it for one minute.
- Now stir in tomatoes, yogurt, 1 tbsp diced cilantro, garam masala, cilantro, 1 tsp salt, chicken breast and half C. of water before bringing all this to boil and cooking on low heat for 20 minutes.
- Sprinkle some lemon juice before serving.

Serving: 6

Timing Information:

Preparation	Cooking	Total Time
20 mins	40 mins	1 hr

Nutritional Information:

Calories	427
Fat	24.3g
Cholesterol	95mg
Sodium	1370mg
Carbohydrates	14.7g
Fiber	2.9g
Protein	38.1g

* Percent Daily Values are based on a 2,000 calorie diet.

☐

SHRIMP

Ingredients

- 2 tbsps peanut oil
- 1/2 sweet onion, minced
- 2 cloves garlic, diced
- 1 tsp ground ginger
- 1 tsp ground cumin
- 1 1/2 tsps ground turmeric
- 1 tsp paprika
- 1/2 tsp chili powder
- 1 (14.5 oz.) can diced tomatoes
- 1 (14 oz.) can coconut milk
- 1 tsp salt
- 1 pound cooked and peeled shrimp
- 2 tbsps diced fresh cilantro

Directions

- Cook onion in hot oil for 5 minutes and let it cool for two minutes before adding garlic, ginger, chili powder, turmeric, paprika and cumin into the pan and cooking it over low heat for a few minutes.

- Now add tomatoes, salt and coconut milk before cooking all this for ten minutes.
- Now stir in shrimp, dried cilantro and fresh cilantro before cooking for one more minute.
- Serve.

Serving: 4

Timing Information:

Preparation	Cooking	Total Time
15 mins	15 mins	30 mins

Nutritional Information:

Calories	416
Fat	32.1g
Cholesterol	146mg
Sodium	930mg
Carbohydrates	10.9g
Fiber	2.9g
Protein	23g

* Percent Daily Values are based on a 2,000 calorie diet.

☐

FRIED POTATOES

Ingredients

- 1 C. vegetable oil for frying, or as needed
- 2 cloves garlic, pressed
- 1 tsp cumin seeds
- 1/2 tsp salt
- 1/4 tsp ground turmeric
- 1/4 tsp ground black pepper
- 5 russet potatoes, peeled and cubed
- 2 tbsps diced fresh cilantro
- 1 tsp mild curry paste (such as Patak's®)

Directions

- Cook garlic, black pepper, cumin, turmeric and salt over medium heat for a few minutes before adding potatoes and cooking for 15 more minutes.

- Now stir in curry paste and some fresh cilantro before cooking for another 1 minute.
- Serve.

Serving: 5

Timing Information:

Preparation	Cooking	Total Time
10 mins	20 mins	30 mins

Nutritional Information:

Calories	268
Fat	4.7g
Cholesterol	0mg
Sodium	267mg
Carbohydrates	52.1g
Fiber	3.8g
Protein	6.3g

* Percent Daily Values are based on a 2,000 calorie diet.

☐

SPINACH AND CHICKEN

Ingredients

- 1 C. diced fresh parsley
- 8 oz. spinach, rinsed and diced
- 1 onion, diced
- 1 potato, cubed
- 4 skinless, boneless chicken breasts
- 6 tbsps olive oil
- 1/4 tsp salt
- 1/4 tsp ground turmeric
- 2 tbsps tomato paste
- 1 C. water
- 3 tbsps fresh lemon juice

Directions

- Cook spinach and parsley in hot olive oil for a few minutes and set it aside for later use.
- Now cook onion in hot oil for a few minutes and then cook

chicken breast in it until brown
from all sides before adding
tomato paste, fried mixture,
water, salt and turmeric.

- Bring all this to boil and let it boil
  for ten minutes before adding
  cubed potatoes and cooking it for
  2 hours.
- Now stir in lemon juice and bring
  the mixture to boil before cooking
  everything for 10 minutes.
- Serve.

Serving: 6

Timing Information:

Preparation	Cooking	Total Time
10 mins	2 hr 20 mins	2 hr 30 mins

Nutritional Information:

Calories	311
Fat	17.7g
Cholesterol	55mg
Sodium	275mg
Carbohydrates	14g
Fiber	3g
Protein	24.9g

* Percent Daily Values are based on a 2,000 calorie diet.

☐

Samosa

Ingredients

- 4 potatoes, peeled and cubed
- 1/4 C. oil
- 2 small onions, finely diced
- 3 tbsps coriander seed
- 1 tbsp curry powder
- 1 (1 inch) piece fresh ginger, grated
- 1 tsp salt
- 1 tsp ground turmeric
- 1 tsp ground cumin
- 1/2 tsp ground allspice
- 1/2 tsp cayenne pepper
- 1/8 tsp ground cinnamon
- 2 roma (plum) tomatoes, finely diced
- 1/2 C. frozen peas
- 4 prepared pie crusts
- 2 egg whites, beaten, or as needed

Directions

- Set your oven at 400 degrees F before doing anything else.
- Cook potatoes in salty water for 20 minutes and mash them.
- Cook onions, coriander seed, turmeric, cumin, pepper, curry powder, ginger, salt, allspice, cayenne and cinnamon in hot oil for 5 minutes and turn the heat off before adding tomatoes and peas into mixture and transferring all this to a bowl containing mashed potatoes.
- Wrap this mixture up in 8 different triangle shaped pie crust and brush it with egg white.
- Bake this in the preheated oven for about 15 minutes.
- Cool it down.
- Serve.

Serving: 16

Timing Information:

Preparation	Cooking	Total Time
30 mins	40 mins	1 hr 40 mins

Nutritional Information:

Calories	315
Fat	18.7g
Cholesterol	0mg
Sodium	396mg
Carbohydrates	32.7g
Fiber	3.9g
Protein	4.9g

* Percent Daily Values are based on a 2,000 calorie diet.

☐

LAMB

Ingredients

- 3 tbsps canola oil
- 1 onion, finely diced
- 4 cloves garlic, mashed
- 1/2 tsp cumin seeds, or to taste
- 1 pound lamb stew meat, cubed
- 3 tbsps tomato paste
- 2 tsps ground coriander
- 2 tsps salt, or to taste
- 2 tsps garam masala
- 1 1/2 tsps ground turmeric
- 1 tsp red chile powder, or to taste

Directions

- Cook cumin seeds, onion and garlic in hot oil for 15 minutes and add lamb, turmeric, tomato paste, coriander, salt, garam masala and red chili powder into the pan before cooking all this for

one full hour or until the meat is
tender.

- Serve.

Serving: 4

Timing Information:

Preparation	Cooking	Total Time
15 mins	1 hr 10 mins	1 hr 25 mins

Nutritional Information:

Calories	242
Fat	15.6g
Cholesterol	53mg
Sodium	1305mg
Carbohydrates	8.1g
Fiber	2.3g
Protein	18.1g

* Percent Daily Values are based on a 2,000 calorie diet.□

EASY PEANUT CHICKEN

Ingredients

- 3/4 C. dry roasted peanuts
- 1/2 tsp paprika
- 1 tsp ground ginger
- 1 tsp ground turmeric
- 1/2 C. honey
- 1/2 C. olive oil
- salt to taste
- 8 chicken thighs

Directions

- Set your oven at 400 degrees F before doing anything else.
- Coat chicken thighs with a mixture of rushed peanuts, honey, paprika, ginger, turmeric, olive oil and salt before refrigerating it for the whole night.

- Place these chicken thighs on the baking dish.
- Bake this in the preheated oven for about 60 minutes, while turning every 15 minutes.
- Serve.

Serving: 4

Timing Information:

Preparation	Cooking	Total Time
20 mins	1 hr	1 day 1 hr 20 mins

Nutritional Information:

Calories	929
Fat	69.4g
Cholesterol	158mg
Sodium	147mg
Carbohydrates	41.6g
Fiber	2.6g
Protein	39.2g

* Percent Daily Values are based on a 2,000 calorie diet.

☐

ALMONDS AND BARLEY

Ingredients

- 1/4 C. butter
- 1 onion, diced
- 1 1/2 C. pearl barley
- 1/2 tsp ground allspice
- 1/2 tsp ground turmeric
- 1/4 tsp curry powder
- 1/2 tsp salt
- 1/8 tsp ground black pepper
- 3 1/2 C. chicken broth
- 1/4 C. slivered almonds
- 1/4 C. raisins (optional)

Directions

- Cook onion and barley in hot butter for five minutes before stirring in allspice, salt, turmeric, curry powder, chicken broth and black pepper, and cooking all this on low heat for 40 minutes.

- Sprinkle some silvered almonds and raisins before serving.

Serving: 6

Timing Information:

Preparation	Cooking	Total Time
5 mins	50 mins	55 mins

Nutritional Information:

Calories	404
Fat	11.1g
Cholesterol	20mg
Sodium	257mg
Carbohydrates	72.5g
Fiber	9.7g
Protein	6.6g

* Percent Daily Values are based on a 2,000 calorie diet.

☐

CHICKEN TIKKA MASALA II

Ingredients

- 1/4 C. plain yogurt
- 2 tsps garam masala
- 2 tsps paprika
- 1/2 tsp freshly ground black pepper
- 1/2 tsp salt
- 1/2 tsp cayenne pepper
- 1/2 tsp ground coriander
- 1 pound skinless, boneless chicken breast - cut into 1-inch strips
- 3 tbsps vegetable oil
- 1 tsp cumin seeds
- 1 large onion, diced
- 3 cloves garlic, minced
- 1 tbsp grated fresh ginger
- 2 green chile peppers, minced
- 2 Roma tomatoes, diced
- 1/2 C. tomato paste
- 1/4 C. water
- 1 tsp garam masala

- 1/2 tsp ground coriander
- 1/2 tsp ground turmeric
- 1/2 C. heavy whipping cream
- 1/2 tsp salt, or to taste
- 1/2 bunch cilantro for garnish

Directions

- Set your oven at 350 degrees F before doing anything else.
- Chicken strips with a mixture of yogurt, 2 tsps garam masala, cayenne pepper, paprika, black pepper, 1/2 tsp salt and 1/2 tsp coriander very thoroughly before refrigerating it for at least two hours.
- Bake these chicken strips in the preheated oven for about 10 minutes.
- Cook cumin seeds for about three minutes and then cook onion for 5 minutes before adding green chili, garlic and ginger, and cooking everything for 20 more minutes.

- Now stir in tomatoes, water and tomato paste, and cook for about 10 minutes before adding garam masala, coriander, turmeric, cream and cooked chicken.
- Cook at low heat for 10 minutes before garnishing with cilantro.
- Serve.

Serving: 6

Timing Information:

Preparation	Cooking	Total Time
20 mins	55 mins	2 hr 15 mins

Nutritional Information:

Calories	403
Fat	25g
Cholesterol	100mg
Sodium	927mg
Carbohydrates	20.5g
Fiber	5g
Protein	27.2g

* Percent Daily Values are based on a 2,000 calorie diet.□

EASY SALMON MASALA

Ingredients

- 2 tsps ground red pepper (cayenne)
- 1/2 tsp ground turmeric
- 1/2 tsp salt
- 1/2 pound wild Pacific salmon fillets, cut into 1-inch cubes
- 2 tsps cornstarch
- 1/2 C. oil for frying

Directions

- Coat salmon with a mixture of salt, cayenne and turmeric, and let it stand for 15 minutes before stirring in some cornstarch and cooking salmon in hot oil for 1 one minute each side.
- Serve.

Serving: 2

Timing Information:

Preparation	Cooking	Total Time
10 mins	5 mins	30 mins

Nutritional Information:

Calories	229
Fat	12.5g
Cholesterol	50mg
Sodium	629mg
Carbohydrates	3.8g
Fiber	0.6g
Protein	24.5g

* Percent Daily Values are based on a 2,000 calorie diet.□

BLACK BEANS

Ingredients

- 1 tbsp olive oil
- 2 onions, finely diced
- 1 bell pepper, diced
- 1 serrano pepper, finely diced
- 4 cloves garlic, mashed
- 1 tsp ground cumin
- 1/2 tsp ground turmeric
- 1/2 tsp cayenne pepper
- 3 tomatoes, diced
- 2 (15 oz.) cans black beans
- 1 (10 oz.) can tomato sauce
- 2 tbsps diced green onion
- 4 tbsps lime juice
- 1 tsp salt
- 1/2 tsp brown sugar
- 3 tbsps diced fresh cilantro

Directions

- Cook onion and in hot oil for five minutes and stir in bell pepper, ground turmeric, serrano pepper, garlic, ground cumin and cayenne pepper before cooking all this for one minute.
- Now stir in diced tomatoes, green onion, black beans, salt, tomato sauce, lime juice, and brown sugar, and bring all this to boil before cooking everything on low heat for thirty minutes.
- Garnish with cilantro before serving.

Serving: 6

Timing Information:

Preparation	Cooking	Total Time
20 mins	40 mins	1 hr

Nutritional Information:

Calories	218
Fat	3.2g
Cholesterol	0mg
Sodium	1186mg
Carbohydrates	39.4g
Fiber	13.3g
Protein	11.2g

* Percent Daily Values are based on a 2,000 calorie diet.

☐

OKRA FROM AFGHANISTAN

Ingredients

- 2 tbsps vegetable oil
- 1 onion, thinly sliced
- 2 tbsps tomato paste
- 1 pound okra, sliced in 1/4 inch pieces
- 1 tsp ground turmeric
- salt and black pepper to taste
- 2 C. water

Directions

- Cook onion in hot oil for 15 minutes and add tomato paste, okra, pepper, turmeric, water and salt before bringing all this to boil and cooking everything on medium heat for 20 minutes.
- Add some salt and pepper before serving.

Serving: 4

Timing Information:

Preparation	Cooking	Total Time
10 mins	35 mins	45 mins

Nutritional Information:

Calories	127
Fat	7.1g
Cholesterol	0mg
Sodium	176mg
Carbohydrates	15.2g
Fiber	5g
Protein	3.3g

* Percent Daily Values are based on a 2,000 calorie diet. □

POTATOES II

Ingredients

- 1 onion, diced
- 1/4 C. vegetable oil
- 1 pound potatoes, peeled and cubed
- 1 tsp salt
- 1/2 tsp cayenne pepper
- 1/2 tsp ground turmeric
- 1/4 tsp ground cumin
- 2 tomatoes, diced

Directions

- Cook onion in hot oil for a few minutes before adding salt, cumin, turmeric, cayenne and potatoes, and cooking everything for 10 minutes.
- Now stir in tomatoes before cooking everything again for 10

more minutes or until you see
that the potatoes are tender.

- Serve.

Serving: 4

Timing Information:

Preparation	Cooking	Total Time
10 mins	20 mins	30 mins

Nutritional Information:

Calories	235
Fat	14.1g
Cholesterol	0mg
Sodium	593mg
Carbohydrates	25.7g
Fiber	4g
Protein	3.3g

* Percent Daily Values are based on a 2,000 calorie diet.

A GIFT FROM ME TO YOU...

Send the Book!

Hey thanks for purchasing my cookbook. If you join my private reader's club you will get one of my favorite books: *A Kitchen in Morocco: Classical Moroccan Recipes.*

This cookbook has over 35 amazing Moroccan and West African recipes that you will absolutely LOVE! It is not available to anyone else, except private readers.

You'll learn how to make classical Moroccan Cous Cous, Peanut Stews, Tagine, Cous Cous Kebabs and a lot more. So join my club!

You will also receive updates about all my new books when they are free. So please show your support.

Also don't forget to like and subscribe on the social networks. I love meeting my readers. Links to all my profiles are below so please click and connect :)

Facebook

Twitter

Google +

REFERENCES

"News Room614-292-5962." *New
Research Adds Spice to
Curcumin's Health-Promoting
Benefits.* Ohio State University,
n.d. Web. 12 Sept. 2015.
<https://news.osu.edu/news/201
4/11/06/new-research-adds-
spice-to-curcumin%E2%80%99s-
health-promoting-benefits/>.

"Turmeric." *Turmeric for Arthritis.* The
Arthritis Foundation, n.d. Web.
12 Sept. 2015.
<http://www.arthritis.org/living-
with-

arthritis/treatments/natural/sup
plements-
herbs/guide/turmeric.php>.

"Turmeric." *University of Maryland
Medical Center*. N.p., n.d. Web.
12 Sept. 2015.
<https://umm.edu/health/medic
al/altmed/herb/turmeric>.

UCLA. "Curcumin." *Curcumin*. Mary S.
Easton UCLA Alzheimer
Translation Center, n.d. Web. 12
Sept. 2015.
<http://alzheimer.neurology.ucla
.edu/Curcumin.html>.

Weil, Andrew. "Q & A Library."
Curcumin or Turmeric? Dr.

Andrew Weil M.D., n.d. Web. 12

Sept. 2015.

<http://www.drweil.com/drw/u/

QAA400915/Curcumin-or-

Turmeric.html>.

COME ON...
LET'S BE FRIENDS :)

I adore my readers and love connecting with them socially. Please follow the links below so we can connect on Facebook, Twitter, and Google+.

[Facebook](#)

[Twitter](#)

[Google +](#)

I also have a blog that I regularly update for my readers so check it out below.

[My Blog](#)

CAN I ASK A FAVOUR?

If you found this book interesting, or have otherwise found any benefit in it. Then may I ask that you post a review of it on Amazon? Nothing excites me more than new reviews, especially reviews which suggest new topics for writing. I do read all reviews and I always factor feedback into my newer works.

So if you are willing to take ten minutes to write what you sincerely thought about this book then please visit our Amazon page and post your opinions.

Again thank you!

INTERESTED IN MY OTHER COOKBOOKS?

For more great cookbooks check out my Amazon Author page:

For a complete listing of all my books please see my author page.

Printed in Great Britain
by Amazon